HEROIN LIES

ACT NOW PLAYS

Series editor: Peter Rowlands
Founding editor: Andrew Bethell

HEROIN LIES

Wayne Denfhy

CAMBRIDGE
UNIVERSITY PRESS

PUBLISHED BY THE PRESS SYNDICATE OF THE UNIVERSITY OF CAMBRIDGE
The Pitt Building, Trumpington Street, Cambridge CB2 1RP, United Kingdom

CAMBRIDGE UNIVERSITY PRESS
The Edinburgh Building, Cambridge CB2 2RU, United Kingdom
40 West 20th Street, New York, NY 10011-4211, USA
10 Stamford Road, Oakleigh, Melbourne 3166, Australia

First published 1991
Fourth printing 1998

Printed in the United Kingdom at the University Press, Cambridge

A catalogue record for this book is available from the British Library

ISBN 0 521 38743 4 paperback

Performance
For permission to give a public performance
of *Heroin Lies* please write to Permissions
Department, Cambridge University Press,
The Edinburgh Building, Shaftesbury Road,
Cambridge
CB2 2RU.

Cover photograph by Aedan Kelly.

ABOUT THE PLAY

Vicki is an ordinary girl. She's no troublemaker or runaway, truant or secret smoker, well, not at first. She reckons she's reasonable looking, but isn't too keen on her ears, or her brother for that matter. She's got an untidy bedroom, likes music and boys, though there's nobody serious at the moment and most of all she enjoys a good laugh with her mates. No, you can't really get away from it, Vicki is incredibly ordinary and it's that that makes her story so frightening.

Heroin Lies is a sensitive and disturbing look at drugs and drug dependency, and in particular the pressures and influences at play on a teenage girl. We observe her gradual and tragic slide towards addiction and also the various degrees of help and hindrance she receives from family and friends.

Guided by a reporter and his nose for a 'good' story, we are slowly drawn into the world Vicki inhabits. It's a recognisable one, populated by real teenagers with real problems, misunderstandings and breakdowns in communication, arguments and laughter . . .

'And you always thought drugs happened to somebody else.' That Vicki's tragedy could have been prevented is a warning to us all!

Go ahead!

'Read all about it! Read all about it!'

CHARACTERS

VICKI BROWN	15, likeable, class clown
JEAN BROWN	Vicki's mother, a worrier
DAVID BROWN	Vicki's father, 'head' of the family
JASON BROWN	17, Vicki's brother
JANE	15, head girl, Vicki's best mate
LINDA	16, the class stirrer
MICHELLE	15, Linda's sidekick
WENDY	15, everybody's favourite joke, manageress of the café
MANDY	15, the new girl
MIKE	16, class poser
COLIN STEVEN	16, Mike's mates
JAMES	15, class wimp
MRS DAVIES	Jane's mother
HEADMASTER	elderly pipe-smoker
CAFE ASSISTANT	
REPORTER	narrator of Vicki's story

THE ORIGINAL SET

The play was originally devised as a Touring Theatre in Education piece, the set for the original production being minimal. It consisted of a number of multi-purpose symbolic objects – a syringe, a bar of chocolate, a lipstick – that could be sat on or stood behind as required.

STAGE DIRECTIONS

There are two kinds of directions in this playscript. Those in **bold type** provide information that is essential to an understanding of what is happening in the play at the time. For a play-reading, these should be read by a separate reader.

Those in *italic type* are less essential stage directions and offer suggestions to assist with a production of the play on stage. In a reading they are best not read out as they will hamper the flow of the play, although those who are reading may find that some of these instructions offer help with the interpretation of their lines.

SCENE 1

Darkness. A heartbeat builds up then fades as the light
comes up on VICKI 's parents. Silence. They sit
uncomfortably in a general hospital corridor. Both are lost
in their own thoughts.

DAVID   Do you want a coffee? (*No reply*) Always a funny smell in
these places . . . sort of antiseptic . . . corridors . . . miles and
miles of blank white corridors . . . why do you suppose they
paint them white?

JEAN   Doctor said he'd be back in ten minutes, that was over half an
hour ago . . .

DAVID   Can't stand waiting . . . never have . . . hate it . . . queues . . .
always seem to . . . pick the wrong window . . .

JEAN   I . . . I just wish I knew what was happening!

DAVID   If they had some sort of system, it'd be something, but no . . .

JEAN   Can't be much longer.

DAVID   . . . Just sit and wait . . . sit and wait.

JEAN   I wouldn't mind a drink or . . .

DAVID   If you're doing something . . . you're occupied . . . your mind
can't wander . . . can't think . . . think if only . . . my old man
used to say they were the saddest words in the world . . . if
only . . .

JEAN   I feel . . . guilty.

DAVID   (*Angry*) Guilt? . . . Don't talk to me about guilt! . . . She knew what she was doing . . . if you're looking for somebody to blame . . . blame . . .

(JEAN **is noticeably upset,** DAVID**'s anger subsides.**)

I . . . I don't mean to . . . it's just I'm a practical man . . . good with my hands . . . can't cope with feeling so useless . . . kids look to good old dad to have a nice neat answer to every problem . . . and I . . . I . . . can't even . . .

JEAN   She's just . . . lying there.

DAVID   Don't!

JEAN   I feel helpless . . . like I've failed her in some way . . . she looks so old . . . so tired . . . she's given up.

DAVID   I don't need this . . .

JEAN   I was thinking . . . last time she was in here was when she had her appendix out . . . six, no seven years of age and for the life of us we couldn't stop her lifting up her dress and showing off her scar . . . sometimes to total strangers . . . oh, she was funny then and cheeky with it! Seems so long ago now . . . like an old film on telly . . . (*Slowly dissolving into tears*) I'm always saying they don't make them like they used to . . .

DAVID   Perhaps . . . er . . . I should get that coffee, now? . . . I'll be back . . . won't be long . . . OK?

(**The** REPORTER, **who in the shadows has been watching the previous action, moves into the spotlight.**)

REPORTER   Read all about it! Read all about it! Tearful tale of a teenage junkie. This story's so hot, the foil's still warm . . . just like your favourite soap opera, but seedier, nastier, sadder . . . The real dirt behind the fingernails. This one will run and run . . . You'll cry till you stop. But I forget myself, ladies and gentlemen. This touching scene of grieving parents you see before you takes place during the tragic conclusion of our torrid tale. Let's start at the beginning . . . turn back the clock, something that poor Vicki could never do!

(**Lights go down on parents. The** REPORTER **leads us to** VICKI, **sitting at her dressing table.**)

Here she is, our front page news . . . to be continued on pages two, five, seven and nine, if blood sports weren't banned! . . . I know what you're saying . . . just an ordinary girl, nothing special. But watch her bleed at your leisure for pleasure, from your favourite armchair, in the safety of your own home! . . . And you always thought that drugs happened to somebody else! . . . Read all about it! Read all about it!

(**The** REPORTER **fades into the background,** VICKI **'comes to life'. She is pulling various faces in front of her mirror, each face slightly modifying her appearance.**)

VICKI   It's me ears you see, too big, like some talking Toby-jug me, quick gust of wind and I'm up in the air, the Human Kite! Course you can do things with them nowadays, get them pinned back like, I'm not sure if I'd be happy with that though, couldn't help thinking that when some hunk was tucking into me earlobe, something back there would snap and they'd spring forward, slapping the poor bloke across the face, like some SS officer . . . Suppose we've all got something about ourselves we don't like, unless you bought your face off a Boot's counter, like *some* girls I could mention, but I won't.

(**She mouths 'Linda Johnson' to the audience, then continues putting on lipstick.**)

Y'know, I sometimes wonder who I'm doing all this for, gettin' myself dolled up that is. I mean is it to make me feel better, or is it to attract some lad? I don't think that's why I do it, I'm not a tart. Nobody notices anyway, except me dad, and he only makes me wash it off! . . . I don't know if Mike'll notice. He's the latest love of my life. He's nothing special, but I just sort of like him. No more than I fancied the last one of course, but that's all part of the game, isn't it? I've got love all figured out, me, all I need now is the bloke. I wonder what the bloke I'm going to marry is doing now . . . right at this moment . . . Probably sitting on the bog . . . or with another woman!

(Laughing to herself she carries on with her make-up.
JASON **walks in. He obviously doesn't come in very often
and is staring round her room.**)

VICKI   Don't you knock?

JASON   What? . . . Oh sorry. (*Knocks on inside of door*)

VICKI   Bit late now . . . What do you want?

JASON   Mum says tea's ready.

VICKI   Finished staring have you?

JASON   Tell me, is that a boy or a girl? (*He points to a poster.*)

VICKI   You should know the difference by now!

JASON   Well it used to be that girls had longer hair, but now I'm not
so sure! (*He notices some of Vicki's trousers.*) You don't wear
these do you?

VICKI   It's called taste, Jason. Something you just wouldn't
understand.

JASON   You won't be able to walk in them.

VICKI   Well they're better than the flares *you* wear!

JASON   Mum bought these!

VICKI   It shows, looks like you're walking round on two hovercrafts!
Cross your legs and somebody across the room gets their eyes
poked out.

JASON   Ha Ha . . . Very funny . . . I've just got more important
things to spend my money on . . .

VICKI   Action man needs a new costume does he?

(VICKI **continues with her make-up,** JASON **picks up some
lipstick.**)

JASON   Why do you waste your money on this stuff?

VICKI   Make myself look beautiful.

JASON   Hasn't worked.

VICKI   You'd look nice wearing make-up you know.

JASON   Come off it!

VICKI   No, straight up! Dab of blusher here, little dash of eye liner there.

(VICKI **collects some make-up and attacks** JASON.)

And a big *puff* of foundation!

(**They struggle amid screams and giggles. Mother enters. They stop instantly.** JASON **is covered.**)

JEAN   What's all this noise then?

VICKI   It's him.

JASON   It's her, tell her!

JEAN   Quiet!! One at a time, now Jason . . . just look at the state of you . . .

VICKI   But Mum!

JEAN   *Jason* will explain what happened.

JASON   I was just sitting here minding my own business and this nutter attacked me with her make-up.

VICKI   That's not right, he asked me to put it on.

JEAN   Is this true Jason?

JASON   No.

JEAN   I think one P.J. Proby is enough for this country to suffer. What would your father say if he knew his son wore make-up?

JASON   But I don't.

JEAN   Well I've heard quite enough from both of you. It's time you started acting your age. Get cleaned up, and get downstairs to that table, your tea's going cold!

VICKI   But Mum, I said I didn't want any tea, I'm meeting Jane at this disco in a quarter of an hour.

JEAN   That's the first I've heard of it, young lady. No excuses, get downstairs and get that tea down you, or you won't be going anywhere . . . and that includes you too Jason!

(Mother leaves. JASON is looking very thoughtful.)

JASON   Vicki?

VICKI   What? . . . If it's about the birds and bees, I haven't got time.

JASON   No. It's not that . . . Vicki, who's P.J. Proby?

SCENE 2

The youth club. Disco lighting. Various characters are spread around the room in small groups. WENDY and JAMES are the only two dancing. JANE is by herself waiting for VICKI. Vicki enters breathless.

VICKI   Hi! Sorry I'm late, had to eat me tea . . . gave rest of it to the cat . . . anything happening?

JANE   He's in!

VICKI   Where? Show us!

JANE   Over there!

VICKI   Where?

JANE   Over there! Behind you! (*She indicates towards Mike and his friends. Vicki begins to turn round. Jane grabs her.*)

JANE   Don't look!

VICKI   How can I see without looking, idiot?

JANE   Pretend you've not seen him. We don't want him to think you fancy him!

VICKI   But I do!

JANE   Yes, but he's not to know that! Do you know your lipstick's on crooked?

VICKI   Is it? Damn! Me dad came in just as I was leaving the house. Made me wash it off again. Had to put it back on on the bus. Conductor didn't half keep giving some dirty looks . . . That better?

JANE   Yeah . . . Who's that with him?

VICKI   With who?

JANE   With Mike.

VICKI   You mean I'm allowed to look over there now, am I?

JANE   Yes, long as you do it subtly.

VICKI   Not like you then! Put your tongue back in . . . Oh that's Steven.

JANE   Steven who?

VICKI   Davies . . . Dunn . . . I'm not sure . . . went out with Linda Johnson for a bit.

JANE   Probably got it, as well!

VICKI   Jane!

JANE   Well, you know what she's like, anything in trousers. No, I can see now he's not my type . . . Have to look elsewhere.

VICKI   What's happened to Tim then?

JANE   We're having a trial separation!

VICKI   You mean you've finished?

JANE   No . . .

VICKI   Come off it!

JANE   Well . . . Maybe . . . Anyway we're not here to discuss my love life!

VICKI   Be a short evening if we were.

JANE   Very funny . . . seen who's over there (*Jane motions towards Linda, Michelle and Mandy.*) Luscious Linda? Must be a full moon. God, she's got some nerve. Just look at that dress.

VICKI   If my dog had a face like that, I'd shave its arse and walk it backwards.

JANE   I think they've seen us (*Nudges Vicki*) Come on, put on your best smile. Wave back!

VICKI   (*Through gritted teeth*) Silly cow!

(Across the room, LINDA and co. wave back.)

LINDA   Lucky escape that, thought for a minute they were coming over.

MICHELLE   No danger of that. Vicki's too busy eyeing up Mike from over there.

MANDY   Does she fancy him then?

LINDA   Can't you tell? She's got no chance of course . . . He goes for the more mature women!

MANDY   He's a grab-a-granny merchant!

LINDA   No, what I mean is that he's been rolling his eyes in this direction all night.

MICHELLE   Hope you picked them up and rolled them back again.

MANDY   Linda's trying to say, in her modest fashion, that he fancies her.

MICHELLE   Didn't you have a snog with him at Jane's party?

LINDA   Yeah, first time he kissed me . . . there was a burning sensation.

MICHELLE   Don't tell me . . . he'd forgotten to take his fag out.

LINDA   You've got it in for me tonight, haven't you!

MICHELLE   No . . . just kidding . . . Have you seen trendy Wendy's new man?

MANDY˙   Bit of a horror, isn't he?

MICHELLE   Reckon he's wearing that tie for a bet?

LINDA   They probably have cosy evenings by the fire, playing join the dots with each other's acne!

MANDY   Go on, I dare you to chat him up.

MICHELLE   I don't know . . . he's not much but he's all Wendy's got.

MANDY   Go on . . . dare you!

(JANE **and** VICKI **move across the room. Vicki dances behind** JAMES.)

MICHELLE   I won't, but here's somebody who might!

(MIKE, STEVEN **and** COLIN **are watching** VICKI's **antics.**)

MIKE   So what did I do next then?

STEVEN   Don't you remember?

MIKE   If I did I wouldn't be asking, would I?

STEVEN   Well you bounded up those steps outside your house like they weren't there, and then you rang the bell with your forehead!

COLIN   Eventually your dad comes out, and you're still ringing the bell – you don't notice him . . .

STEVEN   Even from where I was you could see your dad was going all sorts of funny colours . . . blue . . . red . . .

COLIN   Then you finally notice him . . . give him one of your big stupid grins and say 'Hello, Dad, I'm pissed.'

STEVEN   And barge straight past him!

COLIN   His face was a picture, John was laughing so much he fell in the hedge!

MIKE   God, did I pay for it though . . . felt sick in the night, didn't I? I know, I think I'll throw up out of the window, nobody'll notice. Brilliant idea I thought . . . Seven o'clock next morning I'm woken up by my mother screaming 'Suppose you think that's funny, do you?' Forgotten there was a ledge outside me window, didn't I? Imagine it, all those blackbirds tucking into their second course of diced carrots. Me old man had a hairy fit, had me out there in me pyjamas spraying the roof with his old hose pipe! Never again!

STEVEN   You always say that, until the next time.

MIKE   No this time I mean it . . . Do I remember something about me snogging with Linda?

COLIN   Yep.

MIKE   Oh God, I'll never live it down . . . She's got hairy palms you know!

STEVEN   What's that Vicki up to? (*They look towards Vicki messing about with James.*) Bit much isn't it? James is pretty harmless.

COLIN   Thought you fancied her?

MIKE   Did. She's alright to look at, bit of a child really.

STEVEN   Shame, nice bum.

COLIN   Anyway, what did happen to that garden gnome?

(VICKI **is grabbing hold of** JAMES' **trouser bottoms and shouting things back to her friends.** WENDY **is looking uncomfortable.**)

JAMES   What are you doing?

VICKI   Measuring your flares mate!

JAMES   Oh . . .

VICKI   There, finished . . . That didn't hurt, did it?

JAMES   No, quite enjoyed it really.

VICKI   You dirty old man!

JAMES   You're Vicki, aren't you?

VICKI   Right first time.

JAMES   I used to have a dog called Vicki.

VICKI   You silver-tongued devil, you know how to charm the ladies, don't you. Have to watch him, Wendy, real ladies' man . . . How about us getting together then, James?

JAMES   Oh, I don't know. (*Looking at Wendy*)

VICKI   Doesn't matter about her . . . C'mon, how about it?

JAMES   I . . . (*Wendy leaves.*)

VICKI   That's settled it then, down the Youth Club, Wednesday. It's a date. (*Thumbs up to the girls*) See yer then. (*James exits.*)

(VICKI **returns to her group smiling.** MIKE **is now with them.**)

It's all fixed up, then.

MICHELLE   Vicki, you're terrible.

JANE   I feel sorry for Wendy.

VICKI   She'll get over it . . . it's only a laugh.

JANE   I'm sure Wendy didn't think so.

MANDY   You gonna meet him?

VICKI   No . . . Oh, hello, Mike.

MIKE   Proud of yourself? . . . You're a real KID . . . 'bout time you did some growing up!

(**There is a silence.** VICKI **looks at her friends for help, then runs out of the disco.**)

SCENE 3

Outside the disco.

JAMES   WAIT WENDY! . . . I can explain.

WENDY   Go and explain to Vicki Brown . . . I'm sure she'll understand.

JAMES   WENDY!!

(They pass VICKI in the shadows. The REPORTER steps into the spotlight.)

REPORTER   Poor, poor Vicki. Enjoying yourself? No, don't feel bad about that. Funny isn't it how we gain pleasure from pain. Heard the one about the bloke who walked into a lamp-post . . . see you're laughing already . . . Heard the one about the thick mick, the lazy black and the left-handed lesbian, you'll laugh so hard it hurts!! Or there's the one about the girl who went too far, just wind her up and see her go. Poor Vicki, she's not begun to squirm yet. The man of her dreams thinks she's a kid and she knows he's not too far wrong. Ah well, plenty more fish in the sea, at least she's got a shoulder to cry on.

(JANE comes out and puts her arm around VICKI.)

JANE   What are you doing out here, it's freezing. Come on back in!

VICKI   NO!!

JANE   Oh, come on Vicki . . . he's not worth getting upset over.

VICKI   Nothing to do with him!

JANE   If it's not him, what is it? . . . Come on, tell me, it's no use bottling it up . . . we all make fools of ourselves sometimes . . . Take me just yesterday . . .

VICKI   It's not just sometimes with me though, is it?

JANE   What do you mean?

VICKI   Me, I'm always putting my foot in it . . . and that lot in there . . . Feel a little bored . . . so it's let's set up Vicki time . . . she's alright for a laugh and me like a stupid fool starts dancing to their tune . . . like some daft puppet . . . It's like being a professional comedian. Sometimes I just don't feel funny . . . I like to be alone . . . not the centre of attention.

JANE   Yeah, but you've got a choice.

VICKI   Have I . . . I suppose it's alright for you being head girl and that . . . me, I wonder sometimes . . . if I stopped playing the fool . . . if anybody would notice me . . . Anyway, I didn't see you telling me not to.

JANE   Yeah, well it was funny, but there are limits.

VICKI   You're my friend, why didn't you stop me?

JANE   Look, I'm not staying out here in the cold. Are you coming or not?

VICKI   No.

JANE   Oh, for God's sake Vicki, sometimes you make me so angry!

(JANE **goes. A few moments later** MANDY **comes out.**)

VICKI   What are you, the second babysitter shift?

MANDY   Jane said you were a bit down.

VICKI   Broadcast over the disco, was it?

MANDY   Come on . . . give us a break. I know what it's like, starting new here like I did . . . there are times when it all gets on top of you.

VICKI   I suppose we did give you a hard time.

MANDY   I coped though. I can help you . . . When I feel a bit off, I take some of this. (*Takes out a package*)

VICKI   Come off it, Mandy, I don't want any of that.

MANDY   Are you even sure you know what it is before you start saying what you do and don't want.

VICKI   I know enough, enough to know I don't want it.

MANDY   I don't know what sort of old wives' tales you've been listening to, but they're all lies. Go on, take it. Do you want to feel like this again. Take some of this and you won't have to.

(She forces it into VICKI**'s pocket.)**

VICKI   I don't know.

MANDY   Look, that's good stuff, I wouldn't give it to just anybody. Take it and if you need a friend sometime use it!

VICKI   Just leave me alone, can't you . . . if you were a real friend you wouldn't give me this in the first place.

(VICKI **leaves . . . lights go down.)**

SCENE 4

Vicki's house.

JEAN   Vicki, is that you? (*Vicki enters.*) I could shake you . . . you've had me and your father worried sick . . . Where have you been all this time?

VICKI   Walking.

JEAN   Walking? Is that it? You'd better give me some answers, girl, and quick or you'll feel the back of my hand.

VICKI   No big deal, I've just been walking.

JEAN   Where to? Who with?

VICKI   Oh, it doesn't matter, Mum, I'm home now alright!

JEAN   Alright, how can you be so cool . . . Do you have any idea where your father is at this moment?

VICKI   A Soho strip club?

JEAN   I'm glad you find it amusing . . . for your information he's at the local police station.

VICKI   Oh, Mum . . . Why? . . . Why make all this fuss . . . I've said I'm sorry . . . I just didn't feel like coming home straight away.

JEAN   Didn't feel like coming home, don't want my tea now . . . you're treating this house like a hotel more and more every day.

VICKI   Don't be like that!

JEAN   Didn't you spare us a thought while you were out gallivanting with your friends? Did you think about how *we* were feeling? No, no, I'm sure you didn't. Just typical of your generation, that. Me, me, me, all the time. You want to start thinking about other people for a change. (*A door slams.*) That sounds like your father back, I dread to think what sort of mood he's in!

DAVID   Oh, so you finally made it back then?

VICKI   Dad, I was just going to bed.

DAVID   Sit down. You've got some explaining to do! Now where have you been?

VICKI   I've just been telling mum this.

DAVID   Well you can just tell it again.

JEAN   She's been out walking.

DAVID   I think she can explain it for herself, dear . . . walking with who?

VICKI   Jane, we just felt like walking.

JEAN   Didn't you think about the dangers? You read the papers like anybody else . . . It's so late . . .

DAVID   So you were walking with Jane?

VICKI   Yes.

DAVID   Liar!

VICKI   What do you mean?

DAVID   I've just been round Jane's house. She says you left the disco early.

VICKI   So that's it now is it, spying on me. What a big man spying on his own daughter. Don't you trust me or something?

DAVID   Seems we've just had cause not to.

VICKI   Bet you never had to spy on wonderful Jason.

JEAN   That's not fair, Jason's got nothing to do with this!

VICKI   He's got everything to do with it. Why can't you understand I'll never be like him, so stop comparing me. I'm just getting sick of it. Let me be myself. I can only say sorry so many times.

JEAN   But we do care, Vicki!

VICKI   No you don't, I'm just a disappointment to you, always will be and I hate you for showing that. I hate you!

(VICKI **leaves the room. Her parents look at each other, stunned.**)

DAVID   I wonder what brought that on?

SCENE 5

The REPORTER steps from the shadows.

REPORTER   Dear, dear me! I know what you're saying. If she was my child. (*Sharp intake of breath*) Nothing like your little angel of course, sat in front of *Blue Peter* as I speak, assembling a cruise missile out of yoghurt cartons and sticky-back plastic. You can have them sitting there at your table chewing their meat forty-two times before swallowing, but unless that little bird sends back its messages you don't know what they do when they step out of your house . . . your castle . . . your prison.

     Vicki planned her escape long ago, her little bird was stillborn. Are you sitting comfortably? Vicki discovered cigarettes, then the rot really set in!

(The REPORTER fades back into the darkness. Lights come up on a headmaster's study. There is a knock on the door.)

HEAD   Come in. (*Vicki enters.*) Ah, Victoria . . . take a seat! Now what can I do for you?

VICKI   You sent for me, sir.

HEAD   Oh yes, of course . . . er . . . I . . . a clue?

VICKI   Caught smoking, sir!

HEAD   Ah yes, tut, tut. Now, Victoria, I've been at this school now . . . oh, far too many years to remember . . . In fact I probably taught your parents . . . Yes, I'm certain I did. I often meet parents in the street, you know, and we laugh about the thrashings I gave them. They say Mr Graves, Mr Graves sir, they say, I remember that time you beat me senseless . . . it taught me a lesson, and nothing against these young teachers of today, but we respected you for that, sir. That's what they say, believe you me. The 'silent assassin', that's what they used to call me, on account of the fact that I used to creep up behind them, before braining them across the head! But the point of this, Victoria, and there is a point, a good point, I don't believe in beating around the bush. The point is, is that with all this experience behind me, I'm a past master at spotting somebody who is going off the rails. And that person is you, Victoria Brown. Truancy, smoking and all in the last few months. Now hear this, you're a fit, healthy young lady. You go to a super school, have a thriving house system and you have parents who care for you. I . . .

VICKI No, they don't.

HEAD Pardon me?

VICKI They don't care for me, they just care for my brother.

HEAD Quite . . . er . . . don't be silly, of course they care for you, and as far as Jason goes, you wouldn't go far wrong by taking a leaf out of his book. Now I hope this little chat has been of some use, any problems don't be afraid to knock on my door . . . Right, well, . . . run along then, child . . . I've things to do.

(VICKI **leaves the room.**)

SCENE 6

Typewriter sound. Lights up on the REPORTER, notebook in hand, and MIKE, STEVEN and COLIN. They are taking part in an interview. The reporter doesn't speak, but continually makes notes.

MIKE   Oh yeah, I remember Vicki Brown.

STEVEN   I mean, it doesn't surprise me!

MIKE   She always was a bit strange.

COLIN   (*To Mike*) Fancied you, for a start.

MIKE   Very funny. No, I mean, she was y'know different.

STEVEN   Not one of the crowd.

MIKE   Always seemed to be on her own, y'know.

STEVEN   Even when she was with other people!

MIKE   Looking back, knowing what's happened since, like, I can see how it all started!

COLIN   Bollocks!

MIKE   What?

COLIN   What you saying?

MIKE   Things I remember.

STEVEN   That time at the Youth Club?

MIKE   Yeah.

STEVEN   She was actin' odd that night.

MIKE   Reckon she must have been on them even then!

STEVEN   Must have been!

COLIN   What night?

MIKE   Y'know, when she got off with James what's-his-name.

STEVEN   An' her an' Johnson had a fight over it!

COLIN   Don't remember no scrap!

MIKE   P'haps not a scrap then, but there was an argument!

STEVEN   Anyway, why you being so funny?

COLIN   Well, it's like I can hardly remember anything . . . it was years ago, maybe the odd bit here an' there but you two, you, you've . . .

STEVEN   Got better memories, eh?

COLIN   Too right . . . since this lot turned up, the way you go on you'd think she was your missus or something!

MIKE   So?

COLIN   So . . . so it don't seem right that's all.

MIKE   We're only telling the man what he wants to know.

STEVEN   Yeah.

COLIN   P'haps, but p'haps the way you remember it isn't the way it was, an' I know I'd hate people telling tales about me if . . . if I couldn't answer back for myself!

(Lights fade, leaving the headline slide 'Troubled Teenager Tempted' illuminated. The REPORTER closes his notebook. Blackout.)

SCENE 7

The sweet shop. LINDA obviously works here. MICHELLE, WENDY and JANE are hanging round for the gossip.

MICHELLE So what did he do next, then?

LINDA That's my secret, and for you to dream about!

JANE That means nothing did happen.

LINDA Oh, listen to the Old Ice Queen herself.

WENDY (*With the right accent and manner*) What was that, that Mae West woman used to say 'I was Snow White but I just sorta drifted.'

(They all laugh.)

JANE Wendy, I never knew you were like that!

WENDY Well, there's a lot of things you don't know, isn't there?

LINDA Anyway, as I was saying, back to my love life.

(They all groan. That moment VICKI walks in.)

VICKI Miss some joke?

JANE Not that you'd notice.

LINDA What can I do for you, Vicki?

VICKI Twenty No. 6, please.

LINDA Not sure I can sell you them, not allowed you know, under age.

VICKI   So that's not Chanel 'Benson and Hedges' I can smell wafting off you then, is it?

LINDA   OK, you win, here!

JANE   Didn't know you smoked, Vicki?

VICKI   Haven't long, can I have a word?

JANE   Yeah.

VICKI   I meant over here.

JANE   You can say what you want in front of this lot.

LINDA   We could do with a bit of juicy gossip.

VICKI   (*Whispering*) Look, I'd prefer it if you didn't mention the smoking to my mum. She thinks I've given up, she'd only be upset.

JANE   I'm hardly likely to, am I? I've not been round yours for weeks.

VICKI   No . . . well, thanks anyway . . .

LINDA   Look Vicki . . . A few of us are going on to a disco tonight . . . fancy coming?

VICKI   No thanks.

MICHELLE   Suit yourself!

JANE   Where are you rushing to?

VICKI   I said I'd meet Mandy.

JANE   Seeing a lot of *her* lately.

VICKI   Yeah, well she's alright when you get to know her. Anyway, have to be off.

LINDA   See you, Vicki. (*Vicki exits.*) Doesn't look well, does she? . . . Well, this bloke was telling me . . . what wonderful teeth I had.

WENDY   Like stars.

LINDA   Not exactly.

WENDY   . . . they come out at night.

(They all look at WENDY, **then burst out laughing.)**

SCENE 8

**Vicki's front room. JASON is sitting watching the TV.
It appears to be Playschool. He's smiling.**

TV   And now children, we're going to be big strong trees . . . let's
see you grow . . . come on you at the back there!

**(Looking round the room, JASON begins to attempt the
activity.)**

Let's see those branches reaching out to the sky! Now that's
not very tall is it?

**(JASON jumps on to the settee to gain extra height.
He looks very pleased with himself.)**

That's better, now say hello to Mr Bird!

(The bell rings and he goes to pieces.)

VICKI   (*Offstage*) Jason, answer the door.

JASON   Get it yourself.

VICKI   (*Offstage*) It's Mandy.

JASON   Oh.

**(He changes his opinion totally and goes to the mirror to
check his appearance. When he's happy he opens the door.)**

MANDY   Hello, is Vicki in?

JASON   Yes, she's still getting ready. You can come in and wait if you
like.

MANDY   Thanks.

              (They go to sit down. Jason's very much aware of her but can't think of anything to say.)

              What are you watching, then?

JASON   Playschool.

MANDY   Very educational. Have they done the story yet . . . I like the story . . . Was it through the square or the round window?

JASON   The smashed window.

MANDY   Sign of the times, I suppose . . . myself I was never too sure about Andy Pandy and Loobeloo getting into the same basket . . . you're really watching this?

JASON   No, just got it on for company.

              (MANDY moves up the settee.)

MANDY   Good looking boy like you getting lonely?

              (She puts her hand on his knee.)

JASON   Oh look, little Ted.

MANDY   Never mind little Ted, I'm interested in you. These are lovely trousers. They say flares are coming back in. Where did you get them?

JASON   I think my mum said Oxfam.

MANDY   Jumper from there as well?

              (JASON, sweating, moves further along the couch.)

JASON   Think so! Vicki doesn't like it, says it's like an old man's.

MANDY   What does she know?

JASON   That's what I say!

              (They are now face to face.)

MANDY   Has anybody ever told you, you've got gorgeous eyes?

JASON   I think mum mentioned it once . . .

(JASON **falls off the settee with Mandy on top of him.
At this moment** VICKI **walks in.**)

VICKI   What are you doing with my friends?

JASON   (*Getting up*) Nothing, nothing.

VICKI   Don't you tell me that, you filthy beast. I can't leave you
alone for five minutes, can I?

JASON   I've got to . . . I've got to . . . (*He's already got his coat on.*)
I've got to walk the dog.

VICKI   We haven't got a dog, Jason.

JASON   Well, the cat needs a gallop then . . . Bye. (*He goes. Vicki and
Mandy burst into giggles.*)

VICKI   You shouldn't encourage him!

MANDY   Oh, but he's sweet. Leave him alone . . .

VICKI   I suppose so. What is it you want, then?

MANDY   You know that night I gave you that stuff, have you still got
it?

VICKI   Yes, somewhere. I thought about using it once or twice but
never did. Do you want me to fetch it?

MANDY   If you could. I'm a bit desperate.

(VICKI **goes. We see a totally different** MANDY – **nervous.
When** VICKI **comes back in, she grabs the package.**)

VICKI   No need to snatch.

(MANDY **gets out her lighter.**)

MANDY   Have you got a fiver?

VICKI   A blue one, you must be joking. Me mam should have one in
her holiday tin though.

MANDY   Fetch it!

(VICKI **gets the note, offers it to** MANDY.)

Roll it for us.

(MANDY **starts to heat the heroin.** VICKI **starts to roll the note, then thinks better of it.**)

VICKI Roll it yourself, I don't want to get involved . . . Do you have to do it here? . . . This is my mum's house . . . That's my dad's chair . . . Mandy.

(**She pushes** MANDY. **The powder spills onto the floor. Mandy turns and slaps** VICKI **across the face.**)

MANDY You stupid bitch . . . look what you've done! . . . Help me pick it up . . . You just don't understand . . . You don't realise how much this stuff costs . . . what I had to do to get it.

(**After a short while she calms down.** VICKI **is still holding her face.**)

I'm sorry I didn't mean to hit you . . . It's just . . . I need it so much . . . things seem better . . . bearable. Take some . . . I hurt you . . . feel better, let me help you . . . please . . . take some . . . For me!

(**As the drug is passed to** VICKI **the lights fade.**)

SCENE 9

Outside in the street. JANE **and** WENDY **are looking in windows.** LINDA **and** MICHELLE **enter.**

JANE   That one there!

WENDY   The blue? Oh no.

JANE   What's the matter, don't you think it'll suit me?

WENDY   It's not that, it's just you always pick blue. Why do you always pick blue?

MICHELLE   Matches her varicose veins, doesn't it!

JANE   Hello, didn't see you there.

LINDA   Off anywhere interesting?

JANE   Not really . . . just wandering.

MICHELLE   Didn't see you at the party the other night.

JANE   No, was it good?

LINDA   Great, got absolutely smashed, don't remember a thing.

JANE   I was invited, but I decided to go out with Vicki instead. It was her 16th.

LINDA   She alright? Don't see much of her these days.

WENDY   She didn't turn up!

JANE   I'm sure she must have had a good reason.

LINDA   I'd heard she'd become a bit unreliable.

MICHELLE   Not the only thing I'd heard. (*Linda nudges Michelle.*) What? I'm not saying anything wrong. Jane must know. She's a mate of hers.

JANE   Know what?

LINDA   See I told you, big mouth . . . Nothing!

JANE   No, come on . . . there's obviously something you're dying to tell me.

LINDA   No, it's not worth bothering about, really, probably no truth in it anyway.

JANE   Well, let me be the judge of that!

LINDA   No, don't worry about it!

JANE   C'mon tell me – you know you want to . . .

LINDA   OK, you asked for it . . . her and Mandy are on drugs.

JANE   Oh, is that all!

MICHELLE   What do you mean is that all? If she was one of my mates, I'd be pretty scared!

JANE   You've been watching too much *Grange Hill*. Vicki isn't on drugs.

LINDA   How can you be so sure?

JANE   I know her too well, she just wouldn't.

LINDA   And this faith comes from a friend she stands up. How touching!

JANE   One thing I do know is that whatever the truth of the situation, she's not going to be helped by your dirty mouth, Johnson . . . Look to yourself that's what I say.

LINDA   What does *that* mean?

JANE   You heard. Come on Wendy, I've got better things to do than stand here listening to this rubbish! (*Exit Jane and Wendy.*)

SCENE 10

A quiet corner of the disco. MANDY **and** VICKI **are sitting together.** JANE **enters.**

MANDY   Give us a light . . . Ta . . . I still don't know why you wanted to come down here.

VICKI   I just did . . . fancied coming down to see the children at play . . . Remember that night I got upset over Mike . . . I was so stupid then.

JANE   Hello, Vicki.

VICKI   Hello.

JANE   Didn't expect to see you down here.

VICKI   Couldn't keep away.

JANE   Can I have a word?

VICKI   You've just had five.

JANE   No, I . . .

MANDY   I think she means in private . . . the looks I've been getting all evening you'd think I was the Wicked Witch of the West . . .

VICKI   You don't have to go.

MANDY   It's OK . . . I want another drink . . . Go ahead, Jane . . . She's all yours.

VICKI   Well?

JANE   It's just things I've been hearing.

VICKI   What sort of things?

JANE   Rumours, about you . . . Linda Johnson said . . .

VICKI   You've not started listening to her now, have you?

JANE   No . . . I'd heard talk before she mentioned it.

VICKI   Mentioned what? . . . Don't keep me in suspense.

JANE   They're saying you're on drugs . . . and Mandy started you on them . . . Well, are you?

VICKI   A real friend shouldn't ask you those sorts of questions.

JANE   Yeah? And a real friend sticks up for you without knowing the truth . . . Say you're not, Vicki . . . PLEASE!

VICKI   I'm not . . . I'm not . . . alright? . . . You've heard it from me now, OK?

JANE   Yes . . . You understand . . . I had to ask . . . You know I did.

VICKI   Yes . . . look, I'm sorry about the other night . . . my birthday . . . I just got tied up.

JANE   With Mandy?

VICKI   Yes, with Mandy as it happens . . . We'll have to make another date soon.

JANE   Yes . . . Oh I nearly forgot. This is for you.

(She passes over a package. It's a silver bracelet.)

It's only something little, but I thought you'd like it. There's an inscription too.

VICKI   (*Reads*) To my best friend . . . Jane.

JANE   I had it done a long time ago.

VICKI   Thanks . . . you staying for a drink?

JANE   No . . . I've got to be in . . . Take care.

VICKI   And you . . . and thanks.

(Exit JANE. VICKI is left looking at the bracelet. Fade.)

SCENE 11

The sound of a typewriter. Lights up. MICHELLE **enters,** LINDA **is seated, the** REPORTER **is barely visible in the shadows.**

LINDA   Is it in?

MICHELLE   It's in.

LINDA   Can't wait, I've told them all at work . . . Well?

MICHELLE   I don't think you'll like it.

    (MICHELLE **hands** LINDA **a newspaper.**)

LINDA   Give it here! What page is it on?

MICHELLE   Page three!

LINDA   You're joking!

MICHELLE   Best page for it, I reckon!

LINDA   I dunno what's wrong with you! It's not every day you get in the paper. (*She finds the page.*) What!!!

MICHELLE   Bit of a shock, eh?

LINDA   Oh my God!

MICHELLE   Well, say something!

LINDA   I . . . I don't understand . . . I mean . . . where did they get the photo from? . . . It's not the one he said he was going to put in!

MICHELLE   No, you were showing a bit of leg in that one!

LINDA   Well, there didn't seem any harm in . . . but this!

MICHELLE I've been thinkin' . . . It must 'ave been that time you went in for Miss Wet T-shirt!

LINDA   I was drunk!

MICHELLE Looks like it!

LINDA   But they can't do this . . . can they? I mean what are people going to think?

MICHELLE What the reporter wants them to I suppose!

LINDA   But it's years old . . . I don't look like that now . . . an' anyway, what's it got to do with the story?

MICHELLE The story? . . . Oh, yeah . . . I nearly forgot about that, have a read, go on . . .

(LINDA **looks at the paper. The** REPORTER **steps out of the shadows to read the story.**)

REPORTER Former Beauty Queen Linda Johnson, 27, told today of her teenage friendship with tragic Vicki Brown . . .

LINDA   Seems fair enough!

MICHELLE You came fourth in that competition!

LINDA   *I* know!

MICHELLE Well?

LINDA   Why'd they put me age in?

MICHELLE Dunno . . . always do.

(LINDA **continues to 'read' the paper.**)

REPORTER 'We were friends' said a still attractive Linda 'the way only girls can be . . . if you know what I mean', she winked.

LINDA   What the hell does that mean . . . she winked!

MICHELLE Anything you like, I suppose!

LINDA   I *don't* like it . . . makes me sound a right . . .

REPORTER   Ex-model now spends her days a far cry from the catwalk; she can be found behind her local supermarket's checkout till. But she has no regrets. 'I mean things could have been worse,' she gazed down at her shapely legs in sadness, 'Look what happened to poor Vicki'.

LINDA   I've heard enough of this! . . . It's rubbish . . . I didn't say half of that . . .

MICHELLE   What did you say, then?

LINDA   Can't rightly remember . . . but nothing like that . . . shouldn't be allowed.

MICHELLE   It's total lies, then!

LINDA   Well . . . not really . . . but it's not the truth either . . . I tell yer, it's the last time I buy this rotten paper . . . Huh . . . 'Faded Glamour Queen'. I ask yer . . . disgustin' . . . (*Pause. Linda looks up smiling.*) Mind you . . . I don't look bad though, do I?

(The REPORTER **closes his notebook. Lights fade on headline, 'Faded Glamour Queen's Tragic Friendship'. Blackout.**)

SCENE 12

Jane's home. JANE'S MOTHER **is ironing,** JANE **is half-heartedly reading a girls' magazine.**

MRS DAVIES   Your Auntie Mary rang up this morning, she asked after you. Asked if you were wearing your present.

JANE   What present was that?

MRS DAVIES   You know, dear, that green jumper.

JANE   Oh no, that was awful.

MRS ˙ES   Don't be so ungrateful . . . I'd like you to write a letter to her thanking her for it!

JANE   Oh, I can just see that. 'Dear Auntie Mary, thank you for the green jumper. It's what I've always wanted, it's smashing, people stop me in the street and say "Where did you get that jumper? It makes you look like a gigantic bogey on legs!"'

MRS DAVIES   Jane, really! (*But laughs despite herself*) I suppose it is rather awful.

JANE   (*Collecting her thoughts*) Mam?

MRS DAVIES   Yes, dear.

JANE   You used to have a special mate at school, didn't you?

MRS DAVIES   Oh yes, Shirley Jones . . . great friends we were . . . don't know where she is now . . . last I heard she'd married some really dodgy character . . . Welsh I think he was!

JANE   If she was in trouble . . . would you help her out?

MRS DAVIES   Of course . . . best I could . . . why, where's all this leading to?

JANE   Oh, nothing!

MRS DAVIES   Come on, now you've started!

JANE   Well, there's been rumours about one of my friends.

MRS DAVIES   Well stop right there . . . you don't get anywhere listening to rumours . . . the horrid inventions of idle tongues! Pay no attention.

JANE   These rumours say my friend's on drugs. (*Silence*)

MRS DAVIES   Which particular friend is this?

JANE   Vicki.

MRS DAVIES   Vicki . . . Jean Brown's girl? The one who used to be round here a lot . . . Well I never.

JANE   If these rumours were true . . . how would you go about helping her?

MRS DAVIES   Do you think they're true?

JANE   I'm not sure . . . Vicki says they're not and I would have believed her six months ago . . . but she's changed so much now . . . I can't tell.

MRS DAVIES   Well my advice is to keep well away!

JANE   But you just said not to listen to rumours.

MRS DAVIES   Yes well, if there's only a grain of truth in these I don't want you to have anything to do with her.

JANE   But how's that going to help her?

MRS DAVIES   As far as I'm concerned she got herself into this mess, so she can get herself out too. Keep well away!

JANE   What if she can't help herself?

MRS DAVIES   I just don't want you involved . . . and another thing I don't want her round here again.

JANE   You can't treat her like a leper, ignoring it's not going to make it go away. Just because you turn the TV off when those starving children come on, doesn't mean they don't exist.

MRS DAVIES   Yes, but it means I don't have to look.

JANE   That's horrible . . .

MRS DAVIES   These things are all self-inflicted . . . and that's the final word I want to hear on the matter . . . is that understood? (*They sit in uncomfortable silence.*)

SCENE 13

The REPORTER steps from the shadows.

REPORTER Click! (*He pretends to switch on a TV.*) I'm the man from the gutter press, and I've come to turn you on. Click! Hands up those who haven't crossed the road to avoid the dreaded flag seller. (*He looks round the audience.*) Liars! Click! You don't want famine when you're eating your tea. Click! Oh, look, it's a girl and I think she's drowning. Oh no, she's waving. I can see the silver bracelet and the track marks down her arm. Urgh. Click! This has been a party political broadcast on behalf of the apathy party. Click! Don't forget to switch off before you go to work. (*Laughing, he fades into the shadows.*)

(Lights come up on the library. LINDA, MICHELLE, VICKI and MANDY are sitting round a table.)

LINDA Found any more dirty words in that dictionary?

MICHELLE No . . . none that I can pronounce anyway.

LINDA God, this is boring.

VICKI Can I copy your homework?

LINDA You could have, if I'd done it.

VICKI Oh well . . . I made the effort.

MICHELLE Procra . . . procras . . . procrastination.

LINDA Pardon?

MICHELLE Procra . . . procras . . . I'm not saying it again.

LINDA Didn't sound as naughty as the last one, anyway . . . What was that again?

MICHELLE   I forget. I'll never find it now . . . Stupidest things ever invented these. Use them to look up how to spell words and you gotta know how to spell the word to look it up.

LINDA   That's the marvel of education for you!

MANDY   Don't look now, Vicki, but I think your new-found foster mum just walked in.

(JANE **enters the room and throws something onto the table in front of** VICKI. **It's the silver bracelet.**)

JANE   Recognise it, do you? Course you do, so you'll also know where I found it, won't you?

LINDA   This some sort of 'Twenty Questions' is it?

JANE   You can shut up for a start, Johnson, you hypocrite. You've put so many knives in people's backs you can hang your entire wardrobe. (*They get up to leave.*) That's it – walk off. Don't like hearing the truth, do ya? How about you, Vicki? Fancy some truth? I'm still waiting for my answer.

MANDY   You don't have to justify yourself to her, Vicki. It's your life.

JANE   Oh yes, I forgot . . . your new chum . . . your special friend. I bet you even share the same syringe.

MANDY   Gosh, we have been reading up, haven't we? Miss 'Social Conscience'. What do you expect for this crusade, then? A little 'I Saved an Addict' badge for your Girl Guides uniform?

JANE   At least I never made one.

VICKI   Stop it! Stop it! Stop talking about me as if I wasn't here. I've had enough of that off me parents . . . I don't need it off you.

JANE   Well, answer my question, then.

VICKI   OK . . . OK . . . So I sold it . . . Satisfied now? You said it was nothing much.

JANE   Obviously not.

VICKI   So I hurt you . . . I sold your special present. Sorry. Right, I've apologised. You keep it.

JANE   I don't want it.

VICKI   So you want me to have it? I'm putting it on . . . look . . .
Happy? I'm wearing it.

JANE   And you'll take it off again as soon as you need more money.

MANDY   Put it round her neck and you could use it as a lead . . . I've
heard enough. Coming?

(MANDY **exits.**)

VICKI   What do you want from me, Jane?

JANE   Talk to me.

VICKI   I'm talking to you now.

JANE   Talk to me as if you mean it, like we used to. Why can't you
look me in the face any more?

VICKI   . . . It's not the same . . . I'm not the same.

JANE   It can be like it was before . . . but the start's got to come from
you. You've got to recognise how far down the road you've
gone. It was always me who got carried away, Vicki. Great
schemes I had . . . plans for the future that were bound to fail.
You were the one with your feet on the ground . . . put me
straight . . . made me see sense . . . I'm not doing this very
well . . . but I'm asking you to put yourself straight, with my
help, if you need me. Stop fooling yourself, Vicki . . . please.

VICKI   Out of all of them, you always had the most faith in me . . .
didn't you . . . I don't deserve that much faith . . . can't live up
to it . . . Don't measure me by your standards, Jane . . . 'cos
I'll always fail. I'm not worth getting upset over . . . I'll be
OK. Mandy and me have got this sorted now . . . You just
wait and see . . . But just don't get involved again, or I'll drag
you down with me.

(VICKI **gets up to leave, leaving** JANE **at the table.**)

VICKI   I was going to buy it back, you know.

JANE   Yeah . . . 'course you were . . .

(**Light fades.** JANE **is left by herself.**)

SCENE 14

Typewriter sound. Lights up on the REPORTER, **sitting at a typewriter.** DAVID, JEAN **and** JASON **are in the shadows, a spotlight picking them out individually when they speak.**

REPORTER   I wonder?

JASON   Done more . . . !

JEAN   . . . been stronger . . .

DAVID   . . . the right thing.

REPORTER   Where to appoint blame, that's the trick, pass the buck, point the finger . . . Ah (*typing*), place the burden of guilt!

JASON   She was my sister . . . I should have known . . . understood . . . told somebody . . . done more . . . our parents couldn't know . . . But what could I do? . . . She wouldn't have listened . . . I was only her brother – anyway where could I go for help? . . . There's phone numbers an' that, but would you ring 'em? Would you know what to do? . . . It wasn't as if we were close . . . like we could talk or something . . . but just to stand and watch it was . . .

REPORTER   The coward's way out, new line!

JEAN   Try and start again . . . put it behind us . . . forget . . . but it isn't that easy . . . spent a long time hiding from the truth . . .

REPORTER   Truth hurts . . . no, too corny!

JEAN   You don't want to believe it could happen to your daughter . . . but you've still got to show her you care . . .

DAVID   . . . Teach her a lesson she'll never forget!

JEAN   You start lying to yourself . . . to others . . . strangers . . . that's what we were . . . strangers in our own home . . .

REPORTER   The headline!

JEAN   Sometimes . . . you forget . . . it's easier . . . Is it wrong I should feel that way? . . . If I could have been stronger . . . for her . . . for us . . . but sometimes you can be too strong.

DAVID   I thought I did the right thing . . . I have to believe that . . . Don't you see . . . if I stopped for a moment to . . . to consider that I might have . . . y'know . . . how could I live with myself. You can understand that . . . can't you . . . can't you?

(Flashbulbs go off continually in DAVID, JEAN and JASON's faces. The typewriter sound starts and gets louder. They slowly lift up one hand to protect their faces. A typewriter bell rings.)

REPORTER   Print it!

(Lights down. Headline slide illuminated 'Strangers in Our Own Home'. Blackout.)

SCENE 15

Vicki's house. DAVID and JEAN are sitting down. David is playing with a small package.

JEAN But you don't know for certain, do you?

DAVID This is proof enough . . . explains a lot of the things that have been happening round here lately.

JEAN But it might not be hers . . . might be one of her friends.

DAVID Are you blind, woman? Haven't you looked at her closely recently. I'm surprised she knows what day of the week it is.

JEAN She's had a touch of flu, that's all . . . I don't think you shouting at her is going to help.

DAVID Perhaps I've not shouted enough in the past.

JEAN Can't we phone the doctor? Get some advice.

DAVID Solve it all with a helpful leaflet . . . oh yes, I'm sure. I'm not having outsiders involved. This is a family problem and we'll solve it under this roof.

(The door slams.)

And I don't want you interfering with any of your soft ideas . . . There's only one way to sort this . . . Vicki, come here!

(VICKI **enters.**)

Going upstairs?

VICKI Yes.

DAVID   Well, you won't find them up there.

VICKI   What do you mean?

DAVID   Your mother was doing her weekly tidy of your tip of a bedroom and she found this.

VICKI   You've been through my things?

JEAN   They just sort of fell out . . . I'm sure there's some simple explanation.

DAVID   Well?

VICKI   Well, what?

DAVID   Do you deny this is yours?

VICKI   No. (*The parents look at each other in disbelief.*) What do you want me to do? Lie . . . I've had enough of lies.

DAVID   Haven't you got anything to say?

VICKI   It's funny. From the first time I've always dreaded this moment . . . now it's here . . . I just feel sort of relieved.

JEAN   How could you, Vicki?

VICKI   You'd be surprised how easy it is, mum.

DAVID   I'm still having trouble taking this in . . . Aren't you ashamed? I know I am.

VICKI   I was at first, but after a while things like pride don't seem to matter.

DAVID   And we're supposed to feel sorry.

VICKI   I . . . I . . .

DAVID   Teenage pressures . . . that the excuse eh?

VICKI   I . . . get . . . confused.

JEAN   I was young once.

VICKI   *He* wasn't!

DAVID   I wasn't weak . . . you've been weak, girl.

JEAN   David!

DAVID   And I can't stand weakness.

VICKI   You don't understand . . .

JEAN   We want to understand!

DAVID   I understand well enough.

JEAN   Listen . . . listen!

DAVID   Had to be strong . . . for all of us.

VICKI   Never asked you.

DAVID   I had no choice . . .

JEAN   When did it start?

VICKI   Long time . . . too long ago . . . Mandy came round . . .

DAVID   Here! . . . You took them here?

JEAN   Better than the street . . .

DAVID   You brought that filth into my house.

VICKI   In . . . in your chair.

JEAN   Vicki!

VICKI   Under your nose . . .

JEAN   Vicki . . . it's no good . . .

VICKI   Didn't have a clue . . . your chair . . . the same chair . . . I used to sit on your knee . . . You . . . you couldn't . . . why couldn't you see?

DAVID   (*Cold*) I trusted you.

VICKI   Trust? . . . Trust's no good . . . Why? . . . Why couldn't you help me? . . . (*near to tears*) Why couldn't you help me?

DAVID   I'm going to make you regret the day you started.

VICKI   Hit me . . . hit me, then . . . sure to make me stop . . . you don't care!

JEAN   We've always cared . . . *both* of us.

VICKI   Never showed . . . he's not bothered . . . he's got Jason.

JEAN   I . . . don't understand.

VICKI   Jason . . . Jason!

JEAN   Vicki, I . . .

VICKI   Jason this an' Jason that . . . too many times.

JEAN   You're wrong . . . so . . .

DAVID   Jason would never do this.

JEAN   I can't believe this is happening . . . to our family . . . our daughter . . . must be some mistake.

DAVID   Proof you want is it? . . . I'll give you proof.

(He grabs VICKI's **arm and pulls back her sleeve.)**

Proof! Look . . . look . . . marks! *Now* can you believe, *now* can you see?

JEAN   Oh Vicki . . . Vicki.

(She throws her arms around her daughter, VICKI's **defence drops.)**

VICKI   I'm sorry, mam . . . I'm sorry.

JEAN   How you must have hurt . . . Well, everything will be alright now . . . Mummy's here.

DAVID   What?

(DAVID separates the two roughly.)

I'm having no drug addict in my house . . . get out!

JEAN   David! This isn't the way.

DAVID   Get out!

VICKI   I'm not stayin' . . . not in this doss-hole.

JEAN   David, please!

(JEAN stops DAVID getting to VICKI. They struggle, she falls. Vicki goes to her.)

VICKI Mam!

(DAVID **makes towards** VICKI. **She backs off.**)

Hit women, do you? . . . Fists instead of brain . . . God, I hate you . . . I hate you.

DAVID Just get out.

VICKI Remember . . . you made me what I am . . . think of that on the cold nights . . . you made me what I am.

(**She slams the door.** DAVID **looks at** JEAN, **then exits.** JASON **enters.**)

JASON Mam? . . . Mam? (*No answer. He moves as if to go.*)

I'll get after dad.

JEAN NO . . . No, leave him be.

JASON But . . .

JEAN He's best left on his own . . . to think.

(JASON **is staring.**)

Not . . . seen . . . me cry . . . too . . . often.

JASON No.

JEAN Be alright in a minute.

JASON Does good to cry . . . you say . . .

JEAN Shopping . . . I was going shopping . . . quick tidy 'fore I went . . . do no harm . . .

JASON Mam?

JEAN Normal mornin' . . . like any other . . . never knew how a day could just up an' turn on you.

JASON Mam . . .

JEAN Few hours ago . . . smilin' . . . laughin' even . . . like some fool in paradise.

JASON Mam . . . it's about Vicki, isn't it?

JEAN   You know? . . . Course you know . . . how long?

JASON   A while . . . I . . .

JEAN   Why couldn't you tell us?

JASON   Never . . . never seemed the right moment . . . How can you tell someone . . . Dad . . . something like that . . .

JEAN   You could try!

JASON   I'm sorry.

JEAN   Don't.

JASON   What's going to happen to her, Mam?

JEAN   I don't know . . . I didn't recognise her . . . the girl who was shouting . . . I had her there for a moment . . . but David wouldn't let me . . . She had such anger in her eyes . . . like some wounded animal . . . cornered . . . I don't know if I'll ever see her again . . . isn't that awful?

JASON   Mam . . . I didn't hate her . . . you know that don't you?

JEAN   I know.

JASON   Sometimes the way she went on she . . .

JEAN   We all say things we don't mean . . . (*Silence*)

JASON   Shall . . . I make a cup of tea?

JEAN   (*Distant*) Oh . . . that would be nice . . . cup of tea solves everything . . . solves everything . . . (*Begins to cry.*)

(Lights fade.)

SCENE 16

Some time has passed since the previous scene. MANDY is sitting by herself in a café playing with some sugar.

CAFE ASST.   You in here again?

MANDY   No law against it, is there?

CAFE ASST.   That's every day this week. Never seen anybody make one cup of coffee last so long.

MANDY   Must be a fascinating job if all you do all day is watch me drink. Need lots of qualifications to pour coffee, do you?

CAFE ASST.   Least I can afford to buy more than one cup. Either you buy another or you get out. I'm fetching the manageress in a minute.

(She walks off.)

MANDY   So what? I'll fetch me dad.

(She checks through the change in her pocket, notices VICKI walking past the window. She tries to attract her attention. Vicki comes in.)

MANDY   Vicki! . . . Vicki! . . . It's me, Mandy.

VICKI   Oh, hi, Mandy . . .

MANDY   Sit down . . . Haven't seen you for ages . . . What you doing nowadays.

VICKI   This 'n' that.

MANDY   Still living at home?

VICKI   Sort of . . . My mum keeps nagging me dad to let me go back . . . I do for a while, but he soon gets sick of me . . . Reckon if I was a horse, he'd have me put down. It's funny . . . Jason's been really sweet . . . keeps giving me bars of chocolate . . . read about it in some book somewhere . . . Can't stand chocolate . . . haven't the heart to tell him. What about you?

MANDY   Oh, doing great . . . got a job down London . . . just got back this afternoon. Reckon I'm gonna get promoted . . .

VICKI   That's a nice story . . . something to write home about . . . Might work for some old granny, but not for me. Don't take me for a fool, Mandy . . . I've lived with lies for too long . . . you just keep dreamin'. Got any stuff?

MANDY   No . . . I thought you might.

VICKI   And I thought you called me in to talk over old times.

(The manageress comes over.)

WENDY   Excuse me, but I'm afraid you'll have to move along. We . . . hang on . . . aren't you Vicki Brown.

VICKI   Might be . . .

WENDY   Yes, you are. And you're Mandy Withnall. Don't you remember me, Wendy? You probably know me better as 'trendy Wendy'. I used to hate that name at the time, but it seems quite funny now. What are you girls doing nowadays?

VICKI   We're government artists!

WENDY   Eh?

MANDY   Drawing the dole!

WENDY   Oh, never mind. I'm manageress of this place, done very well, if I say so myself. Notice the ring. Go on . . . have a look. Got a little kid on the way, too.

MANDY   Not James?

WENDY   No. Gosh, no! I married Mike . . . Mike Peters. Remember him. I'm sure you do, Vicki! You had a right crush on him at one time.

VICKI   Did I?

WENDY   Oh, yes! We're very happy . . . got a nice little house on the new estate, company car . . . can't complain . . . Anyway, it's been nice chatting to you, girls. We'll have to do it again sometime. Oh . . . and about the coffee . . . you have that one on me. What are friends for? That's what I say.

(She leaves.)

MANDY   Trendy Wendy . . . who'd have thought . . . Funny thing, your past . . . has a way of catching up with you . . . I don't think I like it . . .

VICKI   What . . . What . . . ever happened to our lives, Mandy? The people we were meant to be . . . Dreams . . . such big dreams . . . going to do everything . . . be a singer . . . would sing out loud into the night . . . Met a famous singer once . . . forget her name . . . She gave me . . . a big, red balloon, I treasured it . . . kept it for weeks . . . till the wind tore it away . . . Tried to grab at it . . . was out of reach . . . nearly out of sight . . . it soared . . . I never stopped singing . . . not inside . . . so high . . . up . . . up . . . like smoke off silver foil.

(Lights fade to darkness.)

SCENE 17

The whole cast are assembled around VICKI **in the darkness. Vicki's face is partly illuminated by a single spotlight.**

VICKI   (*A syringe in her hand*) Know what this is? Syringe . . . Doctors will tell you it puts things in . . . I know different . . . Takes stuff out . . . Don't let them fool you . . . That's full of pride . . . my pride . . . Have to look closely . . . not much left . . . like tears . . . see-through . . . willpower too . . . and love . . . Funny word 'love' . . . don't notice it till it's gone . . . My . . . my . . . dad crossed the street the other day . . . rather than look at me . . . part of him's in there too . . . Mum doesn't go out much now . . . stares out of the window . . . all day . . . waiting for the phone to ring . . . worries a lot . . . about me . . . more than I do . . . about myself . . . Nobody's going to have to worry about me any more . . .

(She injects herself. From this moment on, we enter her drug illusion. All the words spoken by the cast will repeat. They will appear then disappear into the shadows. VICKI **will often have to shout to make herself heard.)**

VICKI   Won't be long now . . .

JEAN   Come to mummy . . . Mummy will make it better . . . (*Repeat*)

VICKI   Mum . . . I'm . . . I'm sorry . . . I couldn't . . . I've let you down . . . I . . . I want . . . to be your little girl again . . .

(She reaches out to her mother, who turns her back.)

JEAN   Vicki, how could you . . . ? (*Repeat*)

JASON   Why do you waste your money on that stuff?

VICKI   I don't Jason, not any more . . . I'm going to get better . . . chocolate bars . . .

MIKE   A real kid . . . 'bout time you did some growing up. (*Repeat*)

VICKI   Mike, I . . .

JANE   You stood me up . . . (*Repeat*)

VICKI   It . . . was . . . only . . . a joke.

JANE   I'm sure Wendy didn't find it funny.

WENDY   Snow White just sort of drifted . . . (*Repeat*)

MICHELLE   What did you do next? (*Repeat*)

HEAD   Jason was such a good boy . . . (*Repeat*)

VICKI   I don't want to be Jason . . . I want to be myself.

JASON   Why do you waste your money on that stuff?

VICKI   I'm . . . I'm not . . . make the world look beautiful.

MANDY   When you need a friend, just use it . . . (*Repeat*)

VICKI   Go away . . . Go away . . . I don't . . . I don't need . . . your sort . . . of friend.

MANDY   Old wives' tales . . . take it. (*Repeat*)

(VICKI **moves to take the drugs.** MANDY **hits her.**)

MANDY   You stupid bitch! (*Repeat*)

JANE   I tried to help you, Vicki, but you wouldn't listen . . . (*Repeat*)

VICKI   A real friend wouldn't . . . I tried . . . but . . . I . . . was always . . . too weak . . . Take me home, Jane . . . Take me home . . .

(**She reaches for** JANE. **MRS DAVIES appears and pulls her away.**)

MRS DAVIES   Keep well away . . . It's all self-inflicted . . . (*Repeat*)

(VICKI **is on her knees. Her father comes out of the shadows, arms outstretched. She moves towards him.**)

VICKI   Dad! . . . I knew you'd understand . . . You'd be there . . . when I really . . . needed you.

(**She's reached her father. His expression changes.**)

DAVID   Get out! Get out! (*Repeat*)

(VICKI **falls to her father's feet. He continues shouting. The rest of the cast begin a mocking laugh.**)

VICKI   Go away! . . . Get out of my head . . . I need . . . to be . . . alone . . . sometimes . . . please . . . Get out!

(**The laughing suddenly stops. Then, very slowly at first, and almost whispered, the whole cast take up the playground chant of 'VICKI's on drugs'. They get louder and louder and more menacing. Vicki screams. Blackout.**)

SCENE 18

Single spotlight on JANE.

JANE   They found Vicki unconscious . . . hunched over on cold concrete . . . in a phone box . . . amongst yesterday's news and broken bottles . . . clutching her bracelet . . . so tight . . . had to prise it from her . . . changed the inscription with an old needle . . . crossed out my name . . . scratched in 'Heroin' . . . She died a few hours later . . . Think it was some sort of message . . . I used to wear it myself until recently . . . Then I had to sell it . . .

The End

WRITING THE PLAY

Who needs another play about drugs? I would have been
inclined to agree with that viewpoint up until a couple of years
ago. That was before a series of drug-related drama lessons with
my fifth-year group.

Although there had been blanket media coverage on the drugs
problem, it seemed that rather than help us understand drugs
more, it had merely created new stereotypes. The shady
anonymous pusher, the drug-taking under bridges or in derelict
houses and the way that drug-taking seemed to be a purely
male-based activity, all these half-truths only obscured the most
important question, why? Why is it that some children take
drugs? It's that question that is central to *Heroin Lies*.

Drug abuse is a strange sort of topic: everybody seems to
think that they know something about it – it nags away at our
national consciousness and titillates us in the national press.
Sadly, there's a sort of dark romanticism attached to it, passed
on by countless generations of dead rock-stars, and yet the most
frightening thing of all remains the disturbing attitude amongst
the general public that drugs, like plane-crashes, happen to
somebody else.

It takes only a little research to reveal the truth: the alarming
number of users who take drugs from friends for the first time,
the high instance of children who take drugs at home and the
wide range of addicts, some as young as nine. It was important
for us that *Heroin Lies* reflect our findings. Vicki had to be
ordinary, somebody the audiences could relate to; and the fact
that nobody really knows what makes an addict surely means
that every child is at risk, and that includes *you*!

Wayne Denfhy

HEROIN LIES – SEE A FRIEND IN TEARS

Words   W. Denfhy   Music   B. Vafidis

Walking barefoot on broken glass
Clouds pass over a watching moon
A telephone box with empty windows
A broken mouthpiece, a waiting queue
A tattered book of distant numbers
Missing pages of a previous life
A final glance in a shattered mirror
Just above where Vicki carved out Mike

CHORUS   *Heroin lies – See a friend in tears*

A number's dialled, hearts still pounding
Hung up when you hear her speak
A mother's voice brings childish memories
You've left the family album incomplete
A mother's tears and a father's anger
Never understands but accepts the blame
A final glance from a frightened neighbour
A mother's loss become a gossip's gain

CHORUS   *Heroin lies – See a friend in tears*

Thoughts of Mandy's smiling eyes
And her pockets packed with hate
Hate that led to this phonebox floor
A shivering world you can't relate
Receiver swings in the dead of night
Pale, perhaps you've stopped breathing
A final glance at a shattered life
Just above which Vicki carved out heroin

CHORUS   *Heroin lies – See a friend in tears*

FOLLOW-UP ACTIVITIES

Note. The end section of this play quite intentionally deals with the underlying issues of behaviours and attitudes that surround the issue of drug use. It was thought inappropriate to use direct addresses on the effects and deprivations of drug use: educational research suggests that confrontational or shocking approaches are not effective in approaching the problem.

Discussion

Vicki, the central character in *Heroin Lies*, meets her death through the abuse of heroin. It is a tragic and pessimistic story which as Wayne Denfhy, the playwright, says in the section 'Writing the play', reflects what can happen to young people who find themselves mixed up in the terrible world of drug-taking. The fact is that we all take drugs of some kind or another at some time in our lives. More often than not we do so for very positive reasons. There can be few of us in the Western world who have not benefited from medicine and remedies that are drug-based. Many of us use drugs socially, drugs such as alcohol, tea and coffee. We may live out long lives without experiencing any really detrimental effects from their use. Often, using such substances makes us feel good in ourselves even though we know that they are destructive for our bodies. One of the most damaging drugs that is used widely, and that is readily available in the corner shop, is tobacco. Each year, thousands of people suffer the pain and indignity of smoking-related diseases which disable and sometimes kill. The abuse of alcohol is a problem because it can not only disfigure the life of the person who drinks too heavily but can have real costs for their families and friends. When mixed with driving, drinking may kill or maim others. Prescription drugs can be abused too, and you have probably read, or maybe know, of people whose lives have become dependent on various drugs.

It is easy to make judgements of other people. Most of us are too quick to say 'It could never happen to me.' And yet it could. The most important lesson to take from *Heroin Lies* and the debate around drug abuse may be that we need to learn to be responsible for our lives and our happiness. Vicki suffers from a terrible self-image. She describes herself as a 'human kite' because her ears are so big. She feels abandoned and uncared for by her family. She is sensitive to being called 'a kid'. Research suggests that nearly all drug abuse, such as smoking or heavy drinking, is related to poor self-image.

The following section offers a number of discussion points around some of the issues in the play. It is probably best to talk about the issues in small groups. One thing to remember is that what you talk about is serious and often personal. Each and every group member needs to be aware of his or her responsibility for taking the issues seriously by listening carefully and sympathetically to what everyone has to say. You also have the right to be heard in the same careful and sympathetic manner.

- On page 14 Vicki makes a remark about someone she is trying to put down and says, 'If my dog had a face like that, I'd shave its arse and walk it backwards.' The exchanges between Vicki and her friends are often like this – smart and sarcastic. Why do you think Vicki does this? What does it do to other people? How does it make her look in the eyes of her friends and feel within herself? Are you aware of the times that you do similar things? What makes you do them? Are your reasons the same as others in the group? Is it easy for people to pay compliments to other people? How do you feel when someone pays you a compliment? What does it feel like to be put down?

- Before beginning this discussion, draw up two columns on a sheet of paper and make a list on one side of all the things that make you feel good or 'high'. Examples could be things like buying new clothes and being smart or fashionable, winning at a game, going for a long walk by yourself, having a bath. In the other column, list the things that make you feel bad or 'low'. Maybe they'll be things like wet days, too much homework, nothing on TV or, yet again, having a bath. When you've done this, share the different lists with members of your group. Does anyone have a 'high' that you call a 'low'? Why do you feel differently about the same thing? Are there people in your group who enjoy the same things but do so for quite different reasons?

  Once you've talked about this for a while, spend some time considering Vicki's life. What things made her feel high or low? What did smoking and heroin do for her self-image? Why do you think she used these drugs? In what way could she perhaps have avoided becoming involved? What high or good things could she have done to have made her feel better about herself as a person?

- On page 39 Vicki is asked by Jane whether the rumours about her taking drugs are true. Vicki replies, 'A real friend shouldn't ask you those sorts of questions.' Do you think Vicki is right? Do you think Jane was right to ask? What other ways may there have been of approaching the problem? The group may like to think about other negative situations people find themselves involved in and whether we have a right to ask questions. What is the difference between being concerned and being nosy?

If you have had the time to involve yourself in the questions raised above, you may like to undertake the following discussion as a whole class.

- How could Vicki's fate have been avoided? In what way could she have taken responsibility for her happiness and well-being? What contributions could other people have made to support her in her day-to-day living? How responsible are Mandy and Jane for what happened in Vicki's life?

Project

Alcohol, cigarettes, and coffee are widely advertised in magazines, on billboards and in the cinema. Alcohol, cigars and tobacco, and coffee are also advertised on television. Spend a week noting examples of this sort of advertising and working out roughly what percentage of all the advertising you see is made up of alcohol, smoking and coffee adverts.

- Select one particular social drug such as alcohol and collect as much advertising material as you can. You may even have access to a video-recorder, in which case you could record advertisements from the television in order to study them.

    Take a close look at how the products are advertised. Some may have a narrative, or story, attached to them. In some instances the story can be quite complex and be part of an advertising campaign that lasts a very long time (years in the case of one instant coffee). Other advertising may lend glamour or status or fun to the product. If people are involved in the images, what sort of people are they? How do they fit into the world that you know and experience every day? What other images/objects are included in the advertisements and what do they suggest? A car could be an example and, if so, is it like the rusting saloon that regularly parks outside your house? Are the interiors of homes similar to the one you are constantly nagged about for leaving untidy? Is the workplace similar to those your friends work at?

Sometimes one advert (text) relies on you knowing about another advert (text) for its effect, often a previous advert promoting the same product. This is known as 'inter-textuality'. An advertising campaign of this sort expects you to pick up on a specific colour, a story-line or a scene which is repeated over a series of adverts. An example would be the use of colour in adverts for some well-known brands of cigarette. There is always a line at the bottom of these adverts carrying a government health warning, but this is the only way the adverts make clear what sort of product they're actually promoting.

Are any of the adverts you chose funny? If so, how does the humour work? Does the humour have anything to do with the product at all?

Having spent some time studying and analysing your area of advertising, see if you can make up your own advertisement using similar techniques to give a quite different message. The meaning that you want to get across to your audience is to warn them that the product has negative effects on lives, or that there are other ways of finding relaxation or a positive feeling about yourself. Try not to make the advertisement seem moralistic, or threatening and full of gloom, but attempt to use glamour, a story-line, humour, or references to other advertisements (inter-textuality) to get your message across.

If you are using a single image in a printed form, you could cut up images and paste them onto a large sheet of paper in a new combination to give you a collage of your fresh advertisement. If you have been looking at television advertising, make up a story-board so that each moment of the advertisement is a still image, much as in a comic. If you've been listening to radio advertising, you could record your advertisement onto a cassette tape.

Writing tasks

When we talk of drug abuse, we often use the words addiction, dependence and habit. It is worth thinking about these words for a moment and deciding what the difference is between them. Is a habit the same as a dependence and is a dependence necessarily an addiction? You may have a habit of biting your

nails. Is this also a dependence? You may depend on the bus
routes and timetables that service your street. Is waiting for the
bus an addiction?

We are dependent in our lives on a great many things other
than drugs. The dependence is not always one that everyone
shares. Some people cannot sleep in a room without a bedside
lamp on. We can become addicted psychologically to things like
eating chocolate, but this is not the same as a physiological
dependence on heroin or nicotine which alters the way the body
works. We can have good habits such as being tidy or kind and
bad habits like being dirty and rude. Human life is also full of
strange and quirky behaviours that make us feel better about
ourselves without damaging our health or affecting the quality
of other people's lives.

- Write a brief story about someone's dependence upon something in
  their lives which for other people looks odd but, for the person
  concerned, makes them feel positive and happy. It could be an old
  lady and her dependence on a loved but mangy cat. It could be a
  child with a favourite toy. Try, in your writing, to give two points
  of view: the point of view of the person with the dependence and
  how it makes her/him feel about her/his daily life and routine; and
  the point of view of someone else who makes a judgement about
  this dependence.
- We all have habits. Some we like and some we hate. Some of our
  habits other people hate. Have you ever sat next to someone in the
  cinema who spent their time cracking their knuckles all the way
  through a really good film?
  Write a letter to an imaginary friend who has a habit that you
  hate, explaining why you don't like this particular behaviour, and
  suggest ways of stopping the habit. Try and make the letter really
  supportive and sympathetic rather than a put-down. Remember
  that habits can have side effects such as stumpy, chewed nails, that
  aren't attractive. Would a nail-chewing friend feel much better
  about her/himself if their hands were attractive?

When people come off drugs after a period of high dependence,
it is called withdrawal. This withdrawal can be very painful. The
side effects of withdrawal from alcohol are known as the 'DTs'
or delirium tremens. It is agonising and can involve physical
convulsions and sweats accompanied by horrible hallucinations.

When withdrawing from drugs, the experience is known as 'cold turkey' and has very similar consequences. Even giving up smoking can be quite physically distressing. Alongside the breaking of a dependence is the loss of a habit. Smokers very often smoke at particular times of the day or after doing certain things. Suddenly these times can seem odd and difficult without the habit. The person may go through a kind of grieving at the loss of something that gave their day some meaning. You may have given up a habit and had much the same feeling of being a bit lost – as if things weren't quite right.

- Choose a habit, either imaginary or real, and write out a plan of a typical day and how that habit fits into all the things that happen. For example:
  7.00 a.m.   Wake up. Reach for cigarettes. Quick fag before going to bathroom for morning cough and wash.
  7.20 a.m.   Downstairs for breakfast of black coffee and a cigarette . . . and so on.
  Having done this, work out a programme for the same day in which the only thing that is missing is the habit. Everywhere that the habit existed, find something positive to replace it with. The positive thing must change during the course of the day, otherwise you will just be replacing one habit with another!
- Write a letter to a friend describing the loss of a friend who has moved to another town. This person was very special to you and you were in the habit of spending large amounts of time together and would jointly do all sorts of things quite regularly. You had got into a *habit* with one another. Now this friend has gone, your days have become quite different. Describe the days before and after the move, and the loss of this friend. Explain how the future may work out and how you will spend your spare time now. Importantly, write about your feelings.

Drama ideas

The following ideas for practical drama are only a few approaches to exploring the themes and ideas in *Heroin Lies*. Really good drama tends to come from the ideas that you have thought of for yourselves, and it may be that sitting down and exploring with one another the issues raised by the play may throw up some things that you want to turn into a practical drama piece.

- In Scene 6, Mike, Steve and Colin are portrayed as adult and are interviewed by a reporter. How they remember events involving Vicki and how these events actually happened are a bit different. You have probably heard similar conversations, in which a little bit of exaggeration has spiced up what actually took place.

  With a partner, (i) work out a quick scene which involves one person tempting the other into taking up smoking; and (ii) work out a second scene, where the person being tempted to smoke in the first scene becomes a teacher interviewing the tempter. Can the tempter twist the truth so that they aren't actually lying about trying to make a friend smoke, yet not quite telling the truth?

- In Scene 8, Vicki has difficulty in saying a straight no to Mandy when she tempts her with the heroin that has been hidden in the house. In the end Vicki is persuaded by the argument that she should 'take some . . . For me!' In what other ways could this have been handled by Vicki? With a partner, take the roles of Vicki and Mandy and see if you can rework the scene so that Vicki can be positive and assertive and say 'No' and mean what is said. The person playing Mandy should try every tactic possible to persuade Vicki that she ought to try the drug.

- Scene 11 finds Linda and Michelle reading a newspaper report of Linda's friendship with Vicki in which the reporter manages to twist meanings and insinuate things by the way in which he writes.

  Work out a group scene involving Vicki and her family discussing her drug dependence. Following this, choose one person to represent the scene by being a reporter giving a spoken television report of what happened in the home. You may wish to show the report to an audience and ask them to guess at the reality before showing them the group scene. Remember, the reporter is unlikely to actually lie. Just stress a few things and sensationalise the issue.

- In Scene 15, towards the end, there is a conversation between Jason and his mother about Vicki and her drug problem. It is revealed that Jason knew about the heroin and was unable to tell his parents. We quite often feel frightened about telling people a particular piece of news. Sometimes this is to protect them. Sometimes to protect ourselves. It is a very understandable state of affairs but sometimes it is important that the news is broken, so that help can be given.

  In a small group, experiment with ways in which Vicki's parents could be told of Vicki's drug problem. Be aware, as you work on this scene, of the feelings of each member of the family.

Often, when someone attempts to suggest to us that something we are doing is wrong, dangerous or harmful, we are tempted to reply that it is our right because it is our life and our risk. But is this always true? Is it just Vicki who is affected by the heroin dependence that she becomes involved with? In the following simulation the issue is whether motorcyclists have the right to decide to ride a motorbike without a crash helmet. Each member of the group should take up one of the suggested roles and then work on the group scenes suggested.

MICHAEL LEVINE	Young motorcyclist enthusiast. Doesn't believe in wearing a crash helmet.
SHARON DORAN	Going out with Michael. Continually suggesting that Michael should wear a helmet.
BETTY and BILL LEVINE	Michael's parents.
GARTH ALLER	A motorist. Suffers from a heart problem.
BOBBY WAITES	A patient waiting for a bed in a men's surgical ward for an operation on his hip.
LINDA WAITES	Married to Bobby. Nursing her husband at home.
CHARGE NURSE MARSH	Nurse in charge of men's surgical ward.
AMBULANCEMAN	
PC FORTE	A policeman.

• Work on a scene between Michael and Sharon about Michael's continual breaking of the law and not wearing a crash helmet. Why does Michael insist on doing this? Why does Sharon object?
• Explore the scene in which Michael has an accident on the road in which he has taken a corner too wide and met head on with a car driven by Garth Aller. Michael is very seriously injured. The police constable arrives on the scene and tells Garth that he is likely to be charged because, although he didn't cause the accident, his tyre treads are too thin. The ambulanceman tells everyone that Michael is unlikely to live because of serious head injuries.
• A brief scene between Michael's parents and Sharon in which they are told by Nurse Marsh that Michael is unlikely to live.
• A scene where Bobby Waites arrives for an operation on his hip, which has been booked for six months, to be told that the bed is no longer available because Michael has taken his place. Linda Waites

is with him and due to take several days' break with her sister
because she is exhausted and run down.
- Michael recovers after all. Everyone in the group should maintain
their roles and meet in a circle to discuss the effect on their lives of
Michael's crash and his head injuries.

Following this short simulation you might like to discuss the
issues that have been raised and how they might apply to Vicki
or to any of us who make decisions that put other people's
happiness at risk. When are such decisions right? When are they
wrong?

Contact addresses

Should you need any form of support or advice about drug
dependence, the following agencies may be able to help you. If
they can't they will most certainly put you in touch with people
who can.

ADFAM (Aid for Addicts and Families)   Tel. 071 823 9313

DAWN (Drugs, Alcohol and Women, Nationally)
Tel. 071 700 4653

FAMILIES ANONYMOUS (support for families and
friends)   Tel. 071 431 3537